I0813337

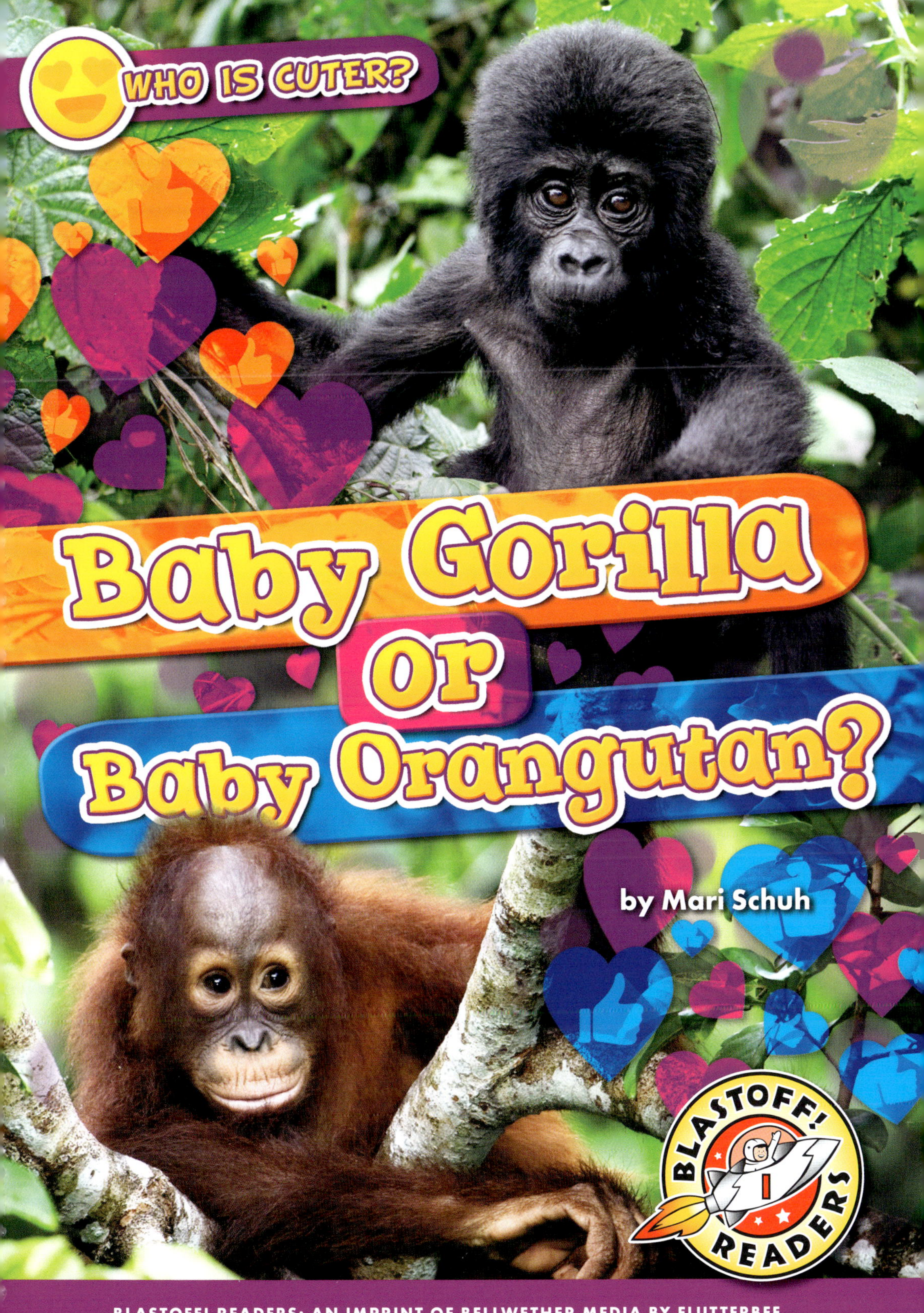

BLASTOFF! READERS: AN IMPRINT OF BELLWETHER MEDIA BY FLUTTERBEE

Blastoff! Readers are carefully developed by literacy experts to build reading stamina and move students toward fluency by combining standards-based content with developmentally appropriate text.

Level 1 provides the most support through repetition of high-frequency words, light text, predictable sentence patterns, and strong visual support.

Level 2 offers early readers a bit more challenge through varied sentences, increased text load, and text-supportive special features.

Level 3 advances early-fluent readers toward fluency through increased text load, less reliance on photos, advancing concepts, longer sentences, and more complex special features.

★ **Blastoff! Universe**

Reading Level

Grade K

Grades 1–3

Grade 4

This edition first published in 2026 by Bellwether Media, Inc.

For information regarding permission, write to Bellwether Media, Inc., Attention: Permissions Department, 3500 American Blvd W, Suite 150, Bloomington, MN 55431.

Library of Congress Cataloging-in-Publication Data is available at www.loc.gov or upon request from the publisher.

ISBN: 9798893047721 (hardcover)
ISBN: 9798893048728 (ebook)

Editor: Rachael Barnes

Printed in the United States of America, North Mankato, MN.

Table of Contents

So Many Infants! 4
Noses and Toes 8
In the Rainforest 14
Who Is Cuter? 20
Glossary 22
To Learn More 23
Index 24

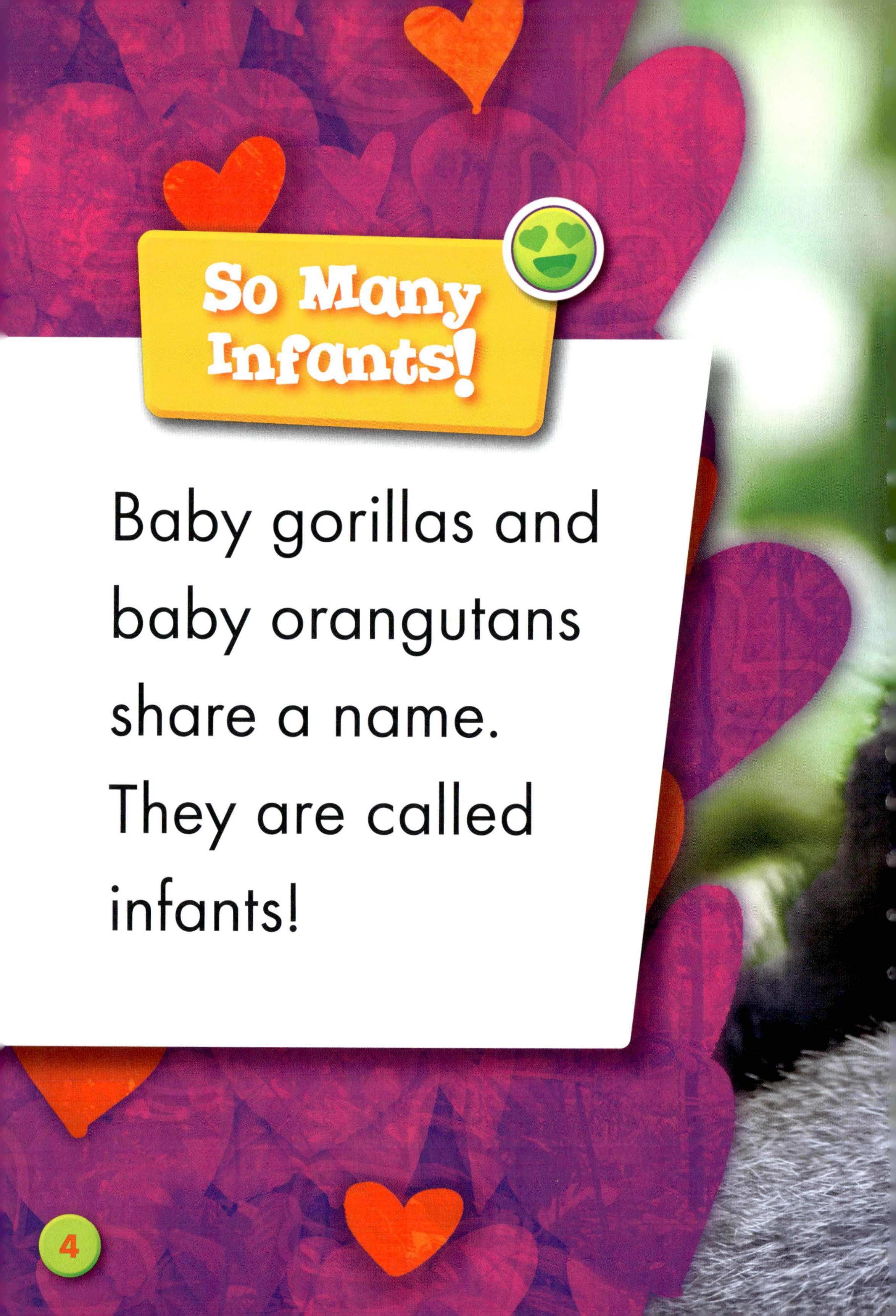

So Many Infants!

Baby gorillas and baby orangutans share a name. They are called infants!

gorilla infant
orangutan infant

Both babies have big bellies. They have long arms. Both are cute!

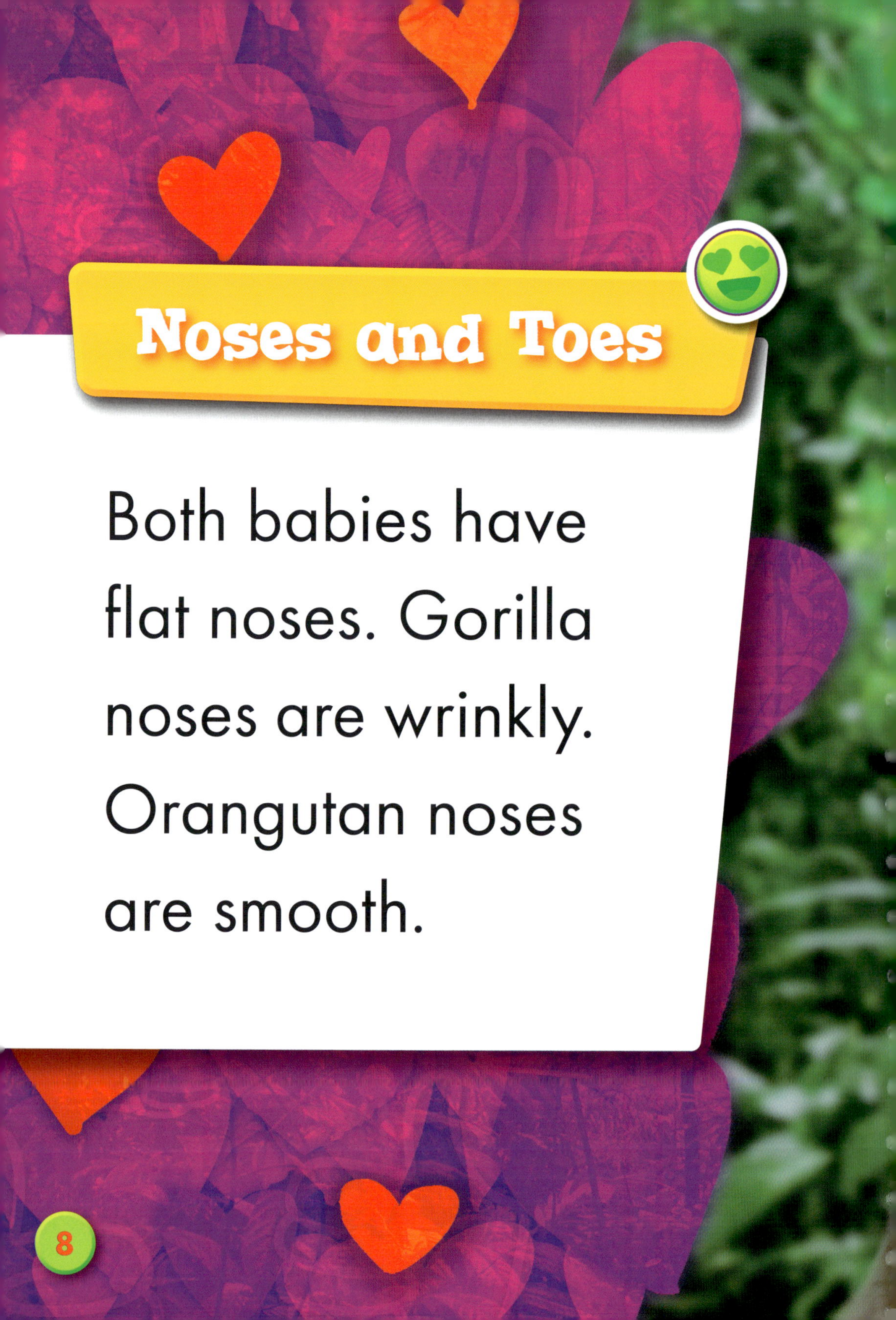

Noses and Toes

Both babies have flat noses. Gorilla noses are wrinkly. Orangutan noses are smooth.

wrinkly
nose

These babies are hairy! Orangutans have orange hair. Gorillas have mostly dark hair.

Orangutan babies have **curved** fingers and toes. Older gorilla babies have strong **knuckles**.

curved fingers
knuckle

In the Rainforest

Both babies live in **rainforests**. Orangutans spend more time in the trees.

The babies learn. Orangutans swing in trees. Gorillas beat their chest.

Gorilla babies giggle. Orangutan babies make a kiss sound. Which baby is cuter?

Who Is Cuter?

flat, wrinkly nose
mostly dark fur
strong knuckles
Baby Gorilla
lives in the rainforest
beats its chest
giggles

Who is your pick?
Vote at
BellwetherMedia.com
flat,
smooth
nose
orange
hair
curved
fingers
and toes
Baby Orangutan
spends
time in
rainforest
trees
swings in
the trees
makes a
kiss sound

Glossary

curved

having a bend

rainforests

thick forests that get a lot of rain

knuckles

bony parts on a gorilla's hands and feet

To Learn More

AT THE LIBRARY

Brandle, Marie. *Gorilla Infants in the Wild.* Minneapolis, Minn.: Bullfrog Books, 2023.

Murray, Julie. *Baby Orangutans.* Minneapolis, Minn.: Pop!, 2024.

Rose, Rachel. *The 10 Cutest Animals.* Minneapolis, Minn.: Bearport Publishing Company, 2025.

ON THE WEB

FACTSURFER

Factsurfer.com gives you a safe, fun way to find more information.

1. Go to www.factsurfer.com.
2. Enter "baby gorilla or baby orangutan" into the search box and click 🔍.
3. Select your book cover to see a list of related content.

Index

arms, 6
bellies, 6
fingers, 12, 13
gorillas, 4
hair, 10
knuckles, 12, 13
learn, 16
noses, 8, 9
orangutans, 4
rainforests, 14
sounds, 18
toes, 12
trees, 14, 16

The images in this book are reproduced through the courtesy of: GUDKOV ANDREY, front cover (orangutan); Ocean Eloy, front cover (gorilla); Fotos 593, background (throughout), p. 22 (rainforests); Eric Isselée, pp. 3 (orangutan), 21 (main orangutan); Edwin Butter, pp. 3 (gorilla), 4-5; Efan Ekananda, pp. 5, 21 (kiss sound); Pitokung, pp. 6-7; Baris Arkin/ Getty Images, p. 7; gnagel, pp. 8-9; jcmarcos, p. 9; Cavan, pp. 10-11; Grantat, p. 11; jwjarrett, pp. 12-13; Riadi, p. 13; Robert, pp. 14-15; McDonald Wildlife Photography Inc./ Getty Images, pp. 16-17; Lukas, p. 17; JFS07, pp. 18-19; BLESKY, p. 19; Nikolay N. Antonov, p. 20 (main gorilla); Rixipix/ Getty Images, p. 20 (lives in rainforest); Joe McDonald, p. 20 (beats chest); Cavan-Images, p. 20 (giggles); Anatoly Alekseev, p. 21 (rainforest trees); Cuson, p. 21 (swings in trees); TravelMedia, p. 22 (curved); Alexandr Junek Imaging, p. 22 (knuckles); MehmetO, p. 22 (gorilla).